The Story Of A Small Boy

By Harvey Starr

"ABOUT LITTLE ROCK"

The Story of a Small Boy

by

Harvey Starr

Considering all the complexities, we could have been so easily passed over. Our presence here is a miracle. We are here today. What would be the odds? Life itself here on this planet earth is a miracle.

Questions remain unanswered as to "Why we are here?" Where did mankind and biological life come from?

There is no roof above us, and in the immense cosmos of space, there is no timepiece. Yet, we are here, today, in the middle of eternity. As human beings, we should celebrate daily, the experience of having lived, especially when we could have been so easily passed over.

Whatever we conceive God to be, in our limited knowledge, is that God was, God is, and God will be. With energy, the physical Universe was created.

Constellations, and all heavenly bodies were spaced far beyond our reach. Secrets understood by only the Maker. Destiny will forever attempt to unlock these mysteries, but we will never fully understand the Magnitude of what God masterfully manages.

Introduction

Little information is available in the genealogy of my Grandparents on my fathers' side of the family. Grandfather Frank Starr met and married Carolina Bernard in Wisconsin, near Racine in the early 1890's. Carolina's family took roots back to the European country of Luxembourg, close to the French Border. Very little else is known about the Bernard Family.

Out of this union, was the family of seven boys, and two girls. By order of birth, there was Phillip, Otto, Frank (my father), John, George, Anna, Ben, Gertrude, and Anton. The three eldest, were born in Wisconsin, whereupon the family moved around the year 1900 to Saint Wendel,

Stearns County, (near Saint Cloud), Minnesota. Later they moved to the Rice area.

The family farmed near the community of Rice, Minnesota in Benton County until 1908, when they moved to their final destination in Buckman Township, Morrison County.

Of my mothers' father's Stellmach Family, they had longer and more traceable roots. However little is known of the "grandmother's genealogy". Her maiden name was Herzing, and little else is known. Dominic Stellmach and Anna Herzing were married around the year 1898, in Rice, Minnesota. From that union, were raised fourteen siblings. By order of their birth, Ben, Susan, Bert, Helen (my mother), Minna, Joseph, Frank, Rose, Clara, Laura, Julius, Genevieve, Clarence, and Florence. Some of my earliest memories are from the event of Grandmother Anna's passing and the funeral that followed a few days later.

The Stellmach genealogy goes back to Western Poland. In Europe, the Rothschilds were financing railroad construction, and supporting financially stronger countries. Austria, France, and Prussia were borrowing large sums of money in paper agreements crafted between the leaders of these countries and the wealthy Rothschild Financial Empire. Russia was invading lands in eastern Poland, and Prussia was squeezing out native Poles from the west, resettling many of its' populace into a region of southwest Poland, called Silesia. The area became hostile and religious intolerance was becoming widespread. The sovereign country that was Poland, was predominantly Catholic, but as civil strife grew, the Bismarck sided with the Protestants of Prussia.

In Silesia, the city of Opole, (Oplan in German) and the surrounding area had been settled and occupied by Catholic grain farmers for years. Due to generally bad conditions, these people were being forced from their homes and land.

At the same time in America, in central Minnesota, a priest from Slovenia, was writing to European Catholic Parishes about opportunities that awaited them in Minnesota. His name was Father Pierz. The City of Pierz, Minnesota is named for him. The people from the general region of Opole started leaving the area in large numbers to come to America.

Stellmach, for some reason, (perhaps it was because he was being conscripted into the Prussian Army (because of his German name) became a fugitive, and sought refuge in the Monastery. The administering Priest, recognizing the desperation, advised Stellmach to flee during the night, and to take with him a young nun, and her sister, a novice, because he feared for their safety, if the soldiers entered the Monastery. The priest released the Sister from her vows and counseled the novice about his fear for their safety due to the civil strife that was going on. He told them to go and make a life for themselves, then gave them his blessing, and what little money he had, then prayed for their safe passage as they left by night. They were forced to hide from the dangers of being caught, until they finally found safety. Several months later, the three boarded a ship, The Saxony, bound for America, in 1865. Upon reaching America, Stellmach and the older of the sisters were married. They had three children, two boys and a girl, after they arrived in America. They had another baby boy. Then later, the mothers' health failed and she died.

Stellmach then married the younger sister, who helped him raise his children. She taught them to speak Polish and German. The second wife gave birth to three more boys and a girl who were half brothers/half sisters to the older siblings. After the second wife died, Stellmach married again, having a single son from the third marriage.

The genealogy then, looks like this:

Coming from Silesia - John, Sr. (great grandfather)

Married first wife, - Catherine

Had four children, Joseph

Francis

Mary

Dominic (my grandfather)

Married second wife, - Francisca

Had four more children -

Walter

Frank

Victoria

John Jr

Married third wife - Johanna

Had one more son - Julius

The German meaning of the word "Stellmach" translates to "Stell = Star" and "Mach = maker". Translated, "Star-maker" in English. The German meaning of "Starr" means "Fixed" or "Firm".

Perhaps the name Starr could have been used as an astronomical term.

The great grandfather is laid to rest in the Gilman Cemetery, and the grandfather, Dominic is buried in the Morrill Cemetery. My Mother died in 1963, and my Father died in 1974. They are buried in the Sacred Heart Cemetery, at Sauk Rapids, Minnesota.

Six boys were born of the union of Frank, Jr. and Helen Stellmach Starr.

By order of birth: Donald (d. 1945)
Vernon (d. 2000)

Ervin	Lives in Sauk Rapids, Minnesota
Harvey	Lives in Yorba Linda, California
Al	Lives in Medford, Oregon
Darwin	Lives in Eden Prairie, Minnesota

My mother and father were special to each other, had similar interests, loved music and enjoyed dancing and traveling. My father was an exceptionally kind man. He went out of his way to treat everyone with fairness while keeping a sense of humor. My mother was a homemaker. She enjoyed sewing, gardening, especially tending to her flowers, and kept very aware of the goings on in the world especially by listening to the radio, and keeping in touch with her brothers and sisters. She was kind, radiant, loving, and thoughtful.

CHAPTERS

One:

A Miracle Begins

Two:

Early Years On The farm

Three:

Strike Anywhere Matches

Four:

Little Pig Market

Five:

The War Years

Six:

Goodbye My Friend

Seven:

Goodbye To An Era

Chapter One: A Miracle Begins

To my many friends, "Perhaps you don't remember me. It has been a very long time!" My first memory of my new life was painful and frightening. I told this to my mother when I was old enough to talk.

She told me of two possible traumatic times in infancy that occurred. One of which I might have remembered and was referring to. "In the moments just after you were delivered from the womb, the attending midwife had much difficulty getting you to start breathing. It took so much time that there was growing concern that they 'might lose the child'."

"I cried, 'give **me** the baby!' and laid the newborn baby on my stomach, and you finally started to breathe!" A miracle? Perhaps, but my mother said, "you surely couldn't have remembered that!" I could tell she was still frightened as she recalled the memory of my birth.

The other incident she spoke of was after an operation to remove an unnatural growth on my right side. "You may well remember coming out of anesthesia after that operation." When Doctor Stein examined me after I was born, he observed a large unnatural growth on the right side of my rib cage. He told my mother, "it must be removed as soon as his health is reasonably stabilized." My mother said I was still quite little when the surgery was performed on my side.

From what I recall, "it felt like I was in a struggle for my life. With extreme pain and accompanied by a distinctive bright light of various colors. I felt as though I was dying." When it finally passed, it seemed like a miracle that I survived that experience. As the weeks and months went on, I saw more and more of Doctor Stein. My first memory of him was more of fear, but later that passed, and I felt some sense of safety with him, as he would examine me and tap me with his fingers. His doctor's office was on the right side of the road as we entered Pierz from the south. We would walk up the steps, and wait in the waiting room to be called. He was a good doctor and still made house calls out to rural areas when it was necessary.

In the hours after my birth, as the doctor examined me, he noted that my head was very badly shaped and lay over to one side all the time as a result of the way the fetus developed in the womb from conception. He counseled my mother to try to work at reshaping the soft skull and try to correct the tendency of my head lying over to one sidc all the time. She tried to prop a pillow and blanket against my head, but when she returned every few minutes, my head was always over to one side.

All my life I have had the natural tendency to want to sleep on the preferred side. I believe my first memory comes to me from coming out of anesthesia after the operation on my right side. My memories after that, of my early days are vivid and clear, almost like a Technicolor Movie.

In the lines that follow, you are invited to join with me on this journey through my childhood. I was born with a passion for life. I have a strong desire to remember all the things that made me who I was, am, and ever will be. I am a part of all that I have seen. My formative years were tutored by events both large and small. These events left an indelible identification in my mind, body and soul. My gratitude is without boundaries to my mother and dad. They were the first ones to teach me how to laugh and be who I am.

They gave me encouragement, and showed me how to "love myself first" so that I may be able to love others fully, without compromise. Their love and kindness to me were simply the best.

It is my hope that you will enjoy reading this adventure as much as I enjoyed writing and describing the days of my early childhood. This is the story of a little boy who had an uncommon enthusiasm and zest for life. I was blessed with an inquisitive, exploring mind, and a heart eager to absorb every tacit of knowledge, with the energy of a locomotive!

Should you be wondering where all this is leading you? Well, you can be sure that this train does not stop here. Read on to find out for yourself, the exciting journey from my infancy, all the way to my twelfth birthday. It all began at "ABOUT LITTLE ROCK".

While in my infancy, I remember many, many things. My mother always marveled at the different things I told her that I remembered. I clearly recall the day my maternal grandmother was buried. Even though I did not comprehend, or have a way to fully relate to the time of the event, I remember when it was and the effect on so many people who left the cemetery deeply mourning.

I recall being in the car. My parents had my brother stay with me in the car during the funeral service, and I wondered, what was taking so long. When all the people started to leave the church, I thought the members of the family would be coming to the car and we would go home. Instead, the large crowd all mingled and seemed to be getting further and further away. As a little person, it seemed like another long time until the people finally started returning to their cars. As the men and women came close past our car where I was waiting, suddenly everything was very quiet. I saw all the people getting into their cars, and they were all sobbing and crying.

I could not quite understand "why" they were all crying, but I knew that it was a symbol of hurt. Most of the ladies seemed to be especially broken up as they had just witnessed a terrible tragedy as they wiped tears from their eyes with their hankies. I remember wondering if they had just come out of some heavy smoke or something else that made them all cry.

After we returned home to the farm, I remember lying on my mother and dads' bed and looking up at the headboard, I noticed a design. If I looked at it one way, it seemed to have a happy smiling face, but looking at the lower part of the image, it appeared angry, and I was frightened by it. When my mother came in to see what I was fussing about I pointed to the image, and she picked me up and laid me in my own crib, where I must have fell fast asleep.

When I awoke, my mothers three youngest sisters were at our house. They stayed with us for several months, and picked me up, held me and fed me. Laura, Genevieve, and Florence all were in their teens, and my mother tried to help them make the adjustment of losing their mother, as they periodically wept, and grieved together.

Some years later, I found my grandmother's headstone on her grave. She passed on in June of 1936. I was born in February, 1934. I quickly calculated that I was just two years and four months old when she died. My mother said, "You couldn't possible remember when my mother died. You were just a baby at the time"! But, I do remember it.

This Stellmach family truly loved each other and one another. They were huggers, and greeted each other with a kiss on one cheek and then the other whenever they came together. Of their traits, I saw they were happy and affectionate people.

My father's family were, generally speaking, more conservative, but deliberate, impeccably honest, and hard working. Perhaps it was because Anna and Gert came along later in the family, the older boys did not display quite the warmth in their social gatherings to begin with. Later, however; as they gathered together, the emotions stirred. Most of the Starr's were brought up to play musical instruments. At birthday parties, and summer events, the members of the family would play and sing. The end result was a huge, happy party. I can remember going home in the car from my uncle George's with music, singing and dancing still going round and around in my head. They knew how to have a party! In the mid 1930's, grandmother Caroline always made sure there were gatherings of the family, especially for the birthdays, Thanksgiving, and Christmas. The Starr's, for being conservative in nature, were particular and exacting in their daily lives. They took nothing for granted, but always had reserves put away, because they remembered how difficult their young lives were.

–

As a little tiny kid, I played under my mother's sewing machine while she sewed. There were trimmings of very colorful cloth, many little pieces of thread and fabric that I would sweep together with my hands, forming little piles. When my mother was finished sewing for the day, she would sweep up the floor along with the little stacks I had made.

While sewing, often, she would have company. There was a neighbor woman, who lived up the road from where we lived. She would walk to our house to visit with my mother. She was old, had gray hair, and used a cane to walk.

I was afraid of her. Her name was Mrs. Schneider. After she arrived, she always wanted to hold me on her lap. I did not want her to hold me or even be near me, but with her cane, she would hook me around the neck and pull me to her, then pick me up and hold me on her lap. My mother knew and realized that I was frightened of her, and would take me from her. Then, wisely, put me back on the floor to play, just outside of the reach of her cane! She might have been the most gentle person in the world, but I was petrified of her and didn't want her to even touch me!

For my birthday, when I was two years old, my mother gave me a pair of new shiny black shoes, and white socks, along with a hard rubber black toy car, which I liked very much. As I played on the floor, my mother listened to the radio as she went about her cooking, and daily routines. She liked the "company of the radio", and the information broadcasts that kept her fully informed out and about in the world. In the spring of 1936, I listened to the radio too, as I played inside the house. I was so very inquisitive and wanted to know everything that was going on around me.

The radio announcers spoke of “kidnapping” and “kidnappers”. They seemed to be repeating it quite often. So to satisfy my curious mind, I asked my mother, “What was so strange about “a kid napping”? She then told me about the little Lindburgh baby that was taken from his bed, and killed. She said the baby was kidnapped, and the bad people who took the baby were “kidnappers”. She said the jury had found and convicted a man they thought did it. His name was Bruno Hauptmann, and they put him to death in the electric chair for the crime, on this day in April, 1936. The nation was divided over the conviction, she said, and many people believed that an innocent man had been put to death. The decision of the jury brought about increased anti-German sentiment around the country. The political nature of the trial, and lack of evidence cast doubt in the minds of many who viewed the proceedings as a "necessity to convict somebody." The trial was held in the city of Flemington, New Jersey, which had become a hotbed for news media and politicians.

Charles Lindburgh was from Little Falls, Minnesota, and was a hero for his transatlantic solo flight in 1927 to Paris, France. The people of central Minnesota were very interested in the outcome of the trial, and were torn between justice being served, and the conviction of a German National for the crime. Central Minnesota being nearly 100 percent German, found it difficult to come to grips with.

The media became more and more critical of Adolf Hitler, who had come to power in 1933, adding to already strained relations. Under Hitler, Germany began nationalizing it's industry and commerce, building it's air force, navy, and army, in defiance of the agreements made at the end of the war in 1918 to the League of Nations.

The stock market crash of 1929 caused much of the world to suffer. By 1936-37, the United States saw boatloads of immigrants again embarking on its' shores. Most of them came with little or few possessions, and as an even greater hardship, could not speak the English Language. One can only imagine how unfriendly the world was at this time.

Unemployment was high. Unions were growing stronger and more hostile. Newly arriving foreigners were willing to work for a fraction of what normal wages had been. Laid off workers resented very much, their jobs being offered to immigrants.

It was in this atmosphere that my parents brought me into the world. Record setting heat greeted me as a small baby in the summer of 1934, and records still stand from that year. Much of the nation especially Oklahoma, Texas, and the southwest became what was termed the "dust bowl".

My father was a farmer. He was also a humanitarian. He would hire unemployed immigrants to help work on the farm, a few at a time. They were mostly from Bohemia, Slovakia, and Poland. My father showed them what he wanted them to do, mostly by hand signals and by his own example. For their hard work, they received a shiny half dollar per day plus room and board.

Because my father was conscripted into the U.S. Army, fought in the Great World War (WWI, in France)*, and was shot, he received a monthly check from the Government. This monthly check, along with the modest amount of money he made from farming, afforded our family "a little more" than most of our neighbors. This was in the depth of the Great Depression, when black bread, and bean soup or potato soup was a standard meal for many.

We lived on a farm, ABOUT four miles from the town LITTLE ROCK, in central Morrison County, Buckman Township, Minnesota. "LITTLE ROCK", taking it's name from the glacial period, when many little stones and little rock spread over the area caused by the glacier from the Ice Age millions of years ago.

Farming on this land was difficult because each spring, before the fields could even be prepared for planting, the rocks had to be picked off the fields. The immigrant hired men worked alongside my father, picking rock and loading them onto "stoneboats" (as they were called), pulled by a team of horses. When loaded full, the horses pulled the stoneboats to a stonepile, where the rock was unloaded, at a remote area of the farm. It was a requirement every spring, because the frost thawing out of the ground would heave a whole new field littered with rock and small stones. Hitting the stones with a plow, seed drill, grain binder, or cultivator was very damaging to field equipment. So the rock in the fields had to be picked. It was hard work, and many of the larger stones had to be dug out with pick and shovel.

Newly arriving immigrants coming to America, looked for work wherever they could find it, and a number of them were glad to pick rock, do chores, and help out around the farm. Most of them were very hard workers. Some did not have any possessions and could not afford even the most basic need. I remember times when someone new would arrive on the farm, and needed work so badly, they would sleep up in the haybarn, or in the granary, until they either moved on or took another worker's place.

My mother cooked for the family as well as the hired workers. Around the table, our conversation was limited, because we could understand only little phrases of what they were trying to tell us. On the farm, there was no shortage of food. My mother made beef roasts, pork, chicken, an occasional goose, a lot of potatoes, crocks of beans, eggs and home made bread. Animals and fowl were slaughtered and dressed as a necessity in order to provide food on a timely basis. Intestines of the hogs were washed and rewashed in salt water to provide casings for specially spiced home-made sausages, which were cooked and smoked along with hams and selected cuts of meat.

Some of the men had relatives in the area, and on Friday nights, they would walk to spend the weekend with the relatives. They would buy cigarettes, a bottle or two of whiskey and go to a Country Dance. When Monday morning came around, they were supposed to be back on the farm ready to go to work. Sometimes they didn't, because they were still drunk. Those who were reliable and worked well were treated accordingly and earned keeps when money was so hard to come by.

On a mild early spring day, just before Easter, my mother dressed me to go outside. Just as she was finishing getting me dressed, she looked out the window and exclaimed; "Oh look! I just saw the Easter Rabbit running around the house! If you hurry, you might be able to see him!" I took off out the door as fast as I could and started to run around the house in search of that rabbit. Lo and behold, I didn't see any rabbit, but I did find a pretty pink Easter Egg lying in a little straw nest alongside the house and it was still warm! I picked up the colored egg and ran back to the front door, bursting with the news that the Easter Bunny had left a colored egg for me! Mother seemed so delighted, and told me to go back out and see if the Rabbit left anymore! So I did, and sure enough, I found two more pretty pastel colored eggs, still warm, one yellow, and the other a pretty light blue.

What a terrific day it was for me! Memories of that day were some of the best a small boy could ever enjoy. Life was so full of joy. Mother's face beamed as she found the fun and excitement she shared with her little boy.

Later in the spring, more and more, I wanted to go outside to play. Most of my outings were cut short by the old gander that was in charge of the geese in our farmyard. A nasty bird! It seemed as soon as the ice melted on the Pond just over the hill to the south of the farm, the geese (a dozen or so) would go for their daily swim. That would be the time for me to be outside in the sun. Being very little at the time, I had to protect myself from that gander. It was like a ritual, every day, off to the Pond they would go. Upon returning, I could hear them a-squawking and honking like they had something really big to tell.

The Gander and I were not friends!

He would come after me with his neck out and his wings close to the ground. He caught me a few times and I can tell you he was mean. I had a real fear of him. So when the geese came back to the farmyard after their daily swim, it meant I had to go in the house. That was the end of my outside playing for the day. This standoff went on for quite a while. I resented that arrogant, dominant goose. I had to figure out a way to outsmart him, even if I had to kill him! One day when I was exploring around the farmyard, I discovered about four cane fish poles hanging on hooks in the car shed where my dad parked the car in cold weather. Well, I climbed up on the front fender of the car. If I could get a fish pole down, maybe I could fight with that gander, then he might leave me alone! It seemed like a plan to engage that nasty old gander! Early next day, I set my plan into place. The geese had gone to the Pond, and I had the fish pole standing up along side the garage next to the grindstone. It wasn't long and I could hear the geese squawking, and saw them coming back to the farmyard. The moment of encounter was arriving, and I was ready!

I took the fish pole, went out into the middle of the yard and waited. With the skinny end of the fish pole in my little hands, I defied that bold bird. He took my challenge as soon as he saw me. With his wings close to the ground, neck feathers sticking out, and hissing, he came charging towards me. I waited for just the right moment. Just as he was getting the proper distance, I swung the big end of the fish pole around full circle, and connected the gander right around the neck!!

The other geese looked on in dismay as the big gander took up a retreat position. I dared him to step into my reach again. The other geese were suddenly very noisy and on about their leaders' retreat. I wished

I could have killed him, but he was a tough old bird.

I was proud of the way I had encountered my adversarial gander. I showed him, he had just met his match, when my mother appeared on the front steps with the broom. She came out to see what was all the noise and commotion.

She immediately saw what was going on. With weapon still in hand, I came running and at the same time I proudly announced, "I almost killed the gander!"

She was not impressed, and with the broom, she took the side of the old bird, (my enemy), and swatted me a good one on the behind. She grabbed the fish pole away from me and told me in the harshest of terms: "You quit fighting with those geese!!"

I was much too young to know it then, but I later figured out, without that gander, there wouldn't be goose eggs that would hatch into little goslings. My mother was just protecting her investment. I still don't like ganders. Left up to me, he would have been a "cooked goose!"

Chapter Two: Early Years on Farm

In February, 1937, I had my third birthday. For the occasion, mother bought me a shiny red rubber ball and a spinning top, which I was finally able to make spin after some practice. She made me feel as though I was the joy of her life. On warmer spring like days, I liked sitting on the little hill just west of the house to watch the airplanes that were training pilots out of Fort Ripley. The planes were mostly old double wingers, with open cockpits. They would fly in "dogfights", rolling and diving, chasing each other. My dad said the Army was training pilots in case they would be needed if we had another war.

My father had a 1931 Pontiac. It was a nice car, dark green, with soft brown-tan, frazee upholstered seats. It was so much fun for me going in the car. Seeing the trees and farms zipping on bye. He traded in that car for a 1933 black Chevrolet, because the Pontiac was hard to start in the winter. The Pontiac had to be started with a crank, and the newer car had an electric starter.

After my dad had the newer car for awhile, he would take it to Nagel's Chevrolet Garage in Pierz, Minnesota for servicing and tuning up. He would leave me in the car when the garage mechanic raised the car up on the hoist. It was quite a thrill and a treat for me because I liked "going up" and looking down at all the interesting things inside the garage.

The biggest thrill of all was when we would go onto the showroom floor and look at the new models. My dad would open the door and put me in the seat behind the steering wheel, and I would pretend to be driving just like my dad!

Going in the car was one of my favorite things to do. During the summer of 1937, when I was about three and one half years old, my parents took me along with them to the city of Little Falls, Minnesota. It was very hot out, and we had all the windows rolled down in the car. When we arrived in Little Falls, we parked just off Main Street. It was a short walk to the busy corner of the main highway (U.S. Highway 10) that intersected the street. Highway 10 was heavily traveled by cars and trucks. When my mother and I arrived at the crossing, she pointed above to a single traffic light that hung high above the center of the road. As the light changed from red to green, a bell rang, to signal the pedestrians and traffic to go across. As we waited our turn to cross, my mom told me we were going to the "Dime Store" where she was going to buy me "a treat". "When the light changes and the bell rings, we have to hurry across, and make sure you hold onto my hand." She said. Upon crossing the street, we entered the corner dime store. It had candy, toys, and all kinds of things for people to look at.

My mom stood at the counter, and a man in a white coat came up and said; "Can I help you, Ma'm." Mother said, "I would like two ice cream cones, one for the little boy and one for myself." With that, the nice man served up the cones, and we left the store.

I never tasted Ice Cream ever before. It was cold and very delicious. Outside on the sidewalk again, the sun was hot. The cold ice cream was so good on a hot afternoon, and I fondly have remembered that day all my life. As we walked, we looked for a place to sit down. My ice cream began to form drips around the cone, and I can still hear my mom telling me "You have to lick faster, and lick around the cone so your hands don't get all sticky!" So I tried to lick faster and licked the drips, turning the cone before it melted and got on my hand. Suddenly, I had a sharp pain in my forehead. I told my mother about how my head hurt. She said it was an "Ice Cream Headache" from trying to eat the ice cream too fast. It was gone in a minute. Meanwhile, the ice cream was melting all over my hands and face, shirt and shoes. As we walked, we came to a Park. There was a water fountain in the park, where my mom cleaned me all up. My mom said I was "a mess from head to toe!"

It was a good thing she got me all cleaned up, because before we knew it, there were two Nuns coming up to talk to us. They had brown "habits" on and what looked like a heavy clothesline cord tied around their waists. They wore white headbands and white bib-like collars circled under their chins, with a black lightweight hood over their head. They were happy, smiling and giggly. They asked me questions, but I was too shy to answer them, so my mom answered them for me. After they spoke to us for a few minutes, they went on their way. My mom said they were "Franciscan Sisters from the Convent and helped care for patients at St. Gabriel's Hospital in Little Falls."

After a few weeks passed, again I got to go along in the car with my mom and dad. This time it was early in the morning and cooler outside. Our trip in the car today would be to

St. Cloud, Minnesota. My dad drove the car to the front of the St. Cloud Hospital, and left us off. The hospital was brand new. My mom was going to visit her sister, Susan, who was a patient there. When we entered into the lobby, a clean, fresh smell greeted us. After getting directions, we boarded the "elevator". It was my first ride on an elevator that took us to the fifth floor. From Aunt Susie's room, my mom held me up so I could see out the window from up so high! Down below I saw the big parking lot. I had never been as high ever before, and it was very exciting for me. After Susan and my mom talked for awhile, we had to say "goodbye and hope you feel better." Walking down the long corridor back to the elevator, two Nuns dressed in glistening white habits approached us. They didn't say anything, but just gave a little nod as we passed them. They looked as much like Angels as anything I had ever seen.

As a little boy, I asked a lot of questions. "Who are they?" I wanted to know. Mother explained, they were "Sisters of the Immaculate Heart of Mary." They too, were working as nurses at the Hospital taking care of the sick.

We then, went down on the elevator, and when we reached the ground floor, the doors opened and guess what, two more Nuns. This time they were all dressed in black habits. They wore a white biblike collar around their front and a white headpiece, with a flowing black lightweight hood, and rosaries hanging from the side of their waists. They were laughing and seemed very happy as they backed up to allow us to get off the elevator. Once again, I wanted to know, "Who are they?" Well, my mother sure knew her Nuns when she identified them as "Sisters of the Order of St. Benedict". She said the "Benedictines" were either Teachers or part of the Administration of the Hospital. They are known as the "Teaching Order of the Church."

The Hospital must have been built in 1936 and completed in 1937. The cornerstone will tell the date. This adventure was before my brother, Al, was born. Al was born on Christmas Day, 1937. A year we didn't get many presents, but on the Eve of Christmas, a Big Jolly Santa Claus in a Bright Red Suit, came to our house, and with bells jingling, he announced his arrival and departure. He gave us candy canes, with red bows and fresh candied popcorn balls.

Many, many years later, I found out who played Santa Claus that night. His name was Martin Miller. Earlier in the year, he worked for my dad as one of the hired men. My dad thought the world of Martin, and being such a warm and comforting man that he was, he made the "perfect Santa Claus". (As I came to know Martin Miller in 1953, he told me how he enjoyed working for my dad for Fifty Cents a day back then.) What a joyful man he was!

The winter of 37 – 38 was cold and harsh, with huge amounts of snow and drifts that were as much as eight to ten feet high. On one morning, after an all night blizzard, my dad tried to open the front door of the house, and the snowdrift was higher than the door which was full of snow. He had to shovel his way out of the house.

With little baby Al's arrival, I could no longer sleep in the little bed across the hall from my parents. Instead, I had to choose which one of my brothers I wanted to bunk up with. I was almost four years old now, and I chose Donald to look after me, over brothers Ervin and Vernon. Donald was my buddy, he took time to play with me and gave me "horsey back rides".

The transition was not nearly as hard as my parents thought, even though the upstairs was unheated and we had to have mounds and mounds of blankets to stay warm. It seemed like Donald was always there to warm me up when I had the shivers. He was my best choice for a new bed partner.

My dad liked to work on projects that offered a bit of a challenge. As my fourth birthday was approaching, he must have found or was given a broken down wooden tricycle, that he thought he could repair and paint up to give me for my birthday. I believe he took it all apart and fixed whatever was broken, repainted all the component parts, and put it away to present it to me for my birthday. When he brought it out, I looked at it- - -I did not like it!

I don't know who was more disappointed, my dad or me. I remember the basic wooden body being red, with small yellow wooden wheels on the back and straight wooden handlebars. The handlebars did not have rubber grips, but just little wooden pegs on each end. The seat and the solid front wheel were painted green and the pedals were made of black hardwood. I was not impressed. I didn't have a thing to do with that trike. One look was all I needed. My parents tried to coax me to "just get on and try it!" - but I would not.

After my parents realized I would never accept it, they took it away and

I never saw it again. I saw pictures in the Sears Roebuck Catalog of the kind of tricycle I wanted. It had shiny chrome handlebars with rubber handgrips. The seat and tubular steel body and back step frame were painted bright red. It had white spoke wheels, rubber tires, with little chrome hubcaps on the back wheels. Now, that was my idea of the kind of tricycle I wanted. I never got another tricycle, it was only a wish or a dream, but it never came true.

During the days just after the repeal of Prohibition, I recall we would have visitors to the farm every few months. What seemed to be different about these visitors, was that they drove a big Black 1937

Studebaker sedan. Another thing was that they were all dressed up in dark suits, topcoats and hats. My dad called them "business people". Whenever they came to the farm, us kids would "OOOooo and Aaaah" about the fancy car. We never knew the reason for them to come to the farm, but they would stay for a while, go here and there with my dad and then get into their car and leave. It wasn't until I was much older that I finally realized dad was selling them "Moonshine" that he had made during the Prohibition.

My father distilled a high quality alcohol. He had his still set up in one of the "out buildings". Whenever he distilled another gallon, he would carefully take the jug off our farm, to "Uncle Tony's place". Tony was the youngest of the Starr family. He owned twenty acres of land just east and across the road from our farm. Uncle Tony never did farm the land, but instead, rented it to my dad year after year. Tony lived in Milwaukee, Wisconsin.

This twenty-acre piece of land had a house on it, but it was never finished inside.

Tony's place was mostly wooded and pasture with only about six acres of tillable land. The property had well water and a big stock tank for the cattle and horses that my dad kept there most of the time. My older brothers and I played in the house many times. Because it was usually closed up, it smelled like lacquer from the untreated wood inside. The house had a good quality wooden floor. Years later, I found out that my dad had a "secret storage" under the floor of the house. This is where he hid his "moonshine". He had a few boards in the floor that were barely nailed. He could easily lift them to hide his alcohol, and replace the boards. Nobody would ever suspect, know, or be the wiser. My dad's good friend, Eddy, was raided and arrested for making moonshine. My dad found out about Eddy, and hastily destroyed his still. None too soon. The next day the Federal Marshals came to my dad's place and tipped the farm upside down, but found nothing. Eddy was sent to Federal Prison for three years for making moonshine. He was released after Prohibition was repealed by Congress.

The Fed's never found the Moonshine my dad had made and hidden under Tony's house. These business people were buying leftover moonshine from my dad as late as 1938, just because he made "good stuff"!

Chapter Three:
Strike Anywhere Matches

In the spring of 1938, after the snow had melted, my dad hired a Painter to paint the barn, silo, granary and all the other "out buildings" on the farm. The paint was a traditional "Barn Red". The painter finished his work ahead of time because of the fair weather. My dad then asked the painter to give everything a second coat on all the buildings. Everything was all fresh and fine, by early May as the painter did his finishing touches. You could smell the fresh paint in the farmyard. The place looked like a million! Everything seemed to be going well. My dad and the hired men were out picking rock in the fields, getting them ready for spring plowing and planting. As the days were getting longer, they stayed out in the fields until well after dark to get a head start on the planting season.

When the hired men came in from the fields at the end of a hard day, they would help do the chores and milking, then wash up at the well, come into the house and have supper with us. After a good meal, these tired hired men would smoke a cigarette or two and fall fast asleep in the chair they were sitting in. Often, with a new freshly opened pack of cigarettes and a few new white cigarettes sticking out of the package opening.

I was obsessed by the smell of the cigarette aroma. I had watched the "lighting up", and those first few, satisfying, draws. It was tempting and fascinating for me! This obsession was strong, and I submitted to the urge to take a cigarette. To my surprise, nothing happened after I took and hid the first cigarette. I was cautious, made sure the hired men were fully asleep. Then only, would I slide another cigarette from the package with the top opened and several cigarettes protruding out so that my little fingers had an easy time at going about my mischief. As the days and weeks went on, I became more and more bold. I took more and more cigarettes and added them to "my collection".

My collection contained every known brand made in the United States. My favorites were Chesterfields, but I didn't care really what kind they were as long as they were accessible. So I "gathered Lucky Strikes, Old Golds, Raleighs, Phillip Morris, Camels, Avalon's, Chesterfields and Wings", took them upstairs and put them in a little box in the bottom drawer of a dresser.

Whenever I would accumulate a third cigarette of a certain brand, I would carefully take it out, and along with a handful of farmer (strike anywhere) matches, would go out behind the granary or one of the other "out buildings". Then light up a smoke with a farmer match. I found it to be very exciting to "light up" and smoke a cigarette like a grown-up. I even learned how to "flick the ashes" by watching the hired men.

I smoked about a cigarette a day for a while, then one day around the

8th of May, 1938, (when I was four years and three months old), I went out for a smoke while my mother was busy washing clothes. It was probably about 2:00 PM in the afternoon, and the weather was just a little blustery. With the wind, I had trouble lighting a match, so I went into the barn.

I decided to strike a match next to the horse stalls to light up my cigarette. As I struck the match, it broke in half, and the lighted end flew into the hay, right under the hay chute! The upward draft immediately sucked the fire right up into the upper hay barn. The fire ignited the dry hay all around me! I could feel the heat from the fire as I turned to see where the side door of the barn was. I had to hurriedly unhook the latch, and when I got out, I ran as fast as my little legs could carry me and alerted my mother. She took one look at the barn, with smoke already billowing from the barn, and ran out in the field to get my dad where he was plowing a field with the tractor. He came running from a distance and headed straight for the burning barn.

He tried from each entrance to free the bull and four or five young stock, but was forced back each time by the intense heat of the fire. The animals were burned alive. It was the most horrible thing I have ever witnessed in my life. As the fire raged on, I wished I could have somehow, some way, "turned back the clock". Neighbors from all around the country- side saw the smoke, and came to try to help, but it was to no avail. The structure burned to the ground.

I felt overwhelming shame for what I did. My parents thought I was playing with matches in the barn. Words cannot describe how much pain I felt, and how sorry I was for what I did. The tragic nature of the loss was even magnified greater, by what I know my dad saw when he tried to save his animals from burning up. His disposition toward all his animals was an attitude of utmost kindness, and he seemed to have an identifiable relationship with all of them. The loss hurt him deeply.

As a little boy, I had intended to light up a Lucky Strike, but it turned out to be a very, very, unlucky strike. I was not punished for what I did. Several days later, in the final resolve,

I went upstairs and took the box of cigarettes, (probably about 30 or so) down and gave them to my dad. I had to tell him that I was stealing cigarettes from the hired men and going outside to smoke them while nobody would see me.

My dad was sad and somber as he lifted the lid from one of the burners of the wood cook stove. He put them into the fire, with me by his side, one by one, until they were all gone.

I never wanted to hurt anyone or anything ever again in my life!

The whole family had to bare the difficulties that were brought on by what I did. All the hardship and extra work I had caused. Particularly, the milking of the cows in the morning and at night with only a makeshift means to keep the cows still as they were milked, one by one. How long could this possibly go on, I wondered?

People came from far and wide to the farm to visit, and would always be determined to seek me out, asking: "Were you the one" (who burned your dad's barn down?) I was compelled to answer in the affirmative. It was a miracle I was not burned up in the fire along with the livestock. My mother and father were just thankful that I was alive!

Our neighbors just to the east of our farm, the Joe Gall Family, were good Samaritans.

They shared our emotions with us. They were also good carpenters, and came over as a family to announce to my dad that they "are going to build a new barn for him."

Joe Gall, and at least six of his sons were committed to volunteer their time and skills, providing my dad bought the lumber and nails, to rebuild the barn. "Old Joe" gave my dad a list of the lumber needed. It was ordered from the Preimesberger Lumber Company in Genola, Minnesota. A few days later a big truckload of lumber arrived at the farm and you would not believe how the rebuilding process accelerated. These honest, hard working, German Catholics, using all hand tools, planned, crafted, and built the best looking barn in all of Central Morrison County! With exceptional know-how and the skills of carpentering brought over from "the old country" (Germany), they put up a barn that still stands today!

During the summer of 1938 after the terrible fire, as the barn was under construction, I spent considerable time with my dad. It was quite a few years later, I found out about how my mother and father "made a pact", whereby, I had to be with my dad and go along every place he went. Baby brother Al, was just five months old on the fateful day of the fire, and it was agreed that mother "could not possibly keep track of four year old Harvey all the time". So my dad began taking me with him everywhere.

I had already given my dad enough grief to last a lifetime.

Besides that, I was "a climber". I climbed to the top of the windmill, up the ladder to the roof of the barn while it was under construction, up on the roof of the granary, and any place else I could climb. I liked to be "up high", so I could see all around the countryside. Many times, my dad would just go and get me down, "before you fall down", he usually said!

I had an uncommon enthusiasm for life, and it was often said of me; "he didn't learn to walk until he was ten years old – because up until then, he ran every place he went!"

As the barn was nearing completion, and summer was heading toward thoughts of back to school, a new air of relaxation and well earned, accomplishment took place. The attitude of everyone was that the worst was now behind us. We began going to see a lot of movies at the "Star Theatre", in Pierz. I went to Genola to the lumberyard, many, many times during the rebuilding and completing of the barn in the summer of 1938.

There were a lot of rumblings about the Germans building up their Military in Europe. At the beginning of the show at the Star Theatre, we saw "Movietone News", showing the precision German Troops in Parade marching in their "Goosestep". As a young lad, the future could be summed up in one word: "Frightening!" My dad often said, "I wonder what really lies ahead?"

Just eighteen years earlier, (1920), my dad came back to the United States on a "Hospital Ship". It was almost two years after the armistice was signed ending the Great War. WWI.

He had been in the US Hospital in Paris recovering from his wounds in July, 1918.

About my Father: He was conscripted into the United States Army after America was drawn into World War I. It was commonly called The Great War, or simply The World War. In the year 1917, he took his basic training at Ft. Lewis, Washington. Upon completion, he had orders to ship to the East Coast by train. From his verbal description, (which I write from memory of a small child), the train left Washington

State, went down through Oregon, into California, along the coast and then east through Arizona, New Mexico, Texas and finally out of New Orleans, headed north through Illinois, Ohio, Pennsylvania and finally New York.

It was a long, tiring trip, taking well over a week by the time they arrived at their staging area. From there, the troops of his unit were sent orders to be transferred to a troop ship for passage to Le Havre, France. These men were part of the contingent to bolster the US Army under General John J. Pershing, who had already arrived in Europe. With the US declaring war on Germany, the US was increasing it's troop strength to oppose the German Army under General Ludendorff and the

Bismarck. The fresh troops were sent through Reims, France on a French Train, and staged for movement into the Argonne Forest, south of Luxembourg, where there had been bitter fighting, and the Allies were not able to advance against the German Front.

Bitter fighting had taken high casualties on both sides as the new contingent started to arrive.

The sound of distant artillery could be heard as the new troops arrived along the woods and hedgerows of what appeared to be an otherwise peaceful and pastoral countryside.

The exact location was in the Ardennes Forest, with the German Army facing the southwest on the high slopes, looking down on the little French Village of Granpre.

Upon arrival, at night, with unbroken silence, the new troops were assembled and given orders. The first mission was to send ten volunteers across the road. The volunteers were reviewed for selection.

Selected, then, it went like this: "You, you, you", and so forth to ten. One of those "you's" was my dad. They were then ordered to cross the road, first one, then two more, then another, and another two, to see if they would "draw fire" from the Germans. This would be to locate where the emplacements were.

The first one crossed the road uneventful. Two more crossed, and they lay in prone position, still no effect. Two more ran across the road, and as they were hitting the ditch on the other side, the German Machine Gun opened fire, and one of the bullets had my dad's name on it. My dad did not realize at first that he had been hit. The sensation he described was that he thought he had fallen onto a sharp stick as he hit the ground, and it "felt hot". He immediately "noticed something wet", and realized, seeing blood, that he had been shot.

The machine gun bullet hit him just below his left temple and went through his soft tissue at an angle, taking out his top back teeth, and sizzling through his tongue, impacting his lower right back teeth. The bullet passed just under his right jawbone and came out in his neck about an inch from his juggler vein.

Fear seized him. . . . . as he lay in the ditch bleeding. A fierce battle broke out with the eventual destroying of the German gun placement. Finally my father was discovered. He was taken from the front lines, and transferred along with other wounded to a Red Cross field hospital. After seeing the extent of his wounds, he was taken to the American Hospital in Paris. For him the war was over. In those brief minutes, he served his country and now the healing would begin.

Because his mouth was all torn up inside, the nurses had no way to feed him. Intravenous feeding was not yet invented. If he could not take food to sustain his body, his strength would fail and he would become vulnerable to infection, due to starvation. In order to get food into his stomach, the nurses had to work with him to have straws put up into his nostrils, and worked down into his stomach. He would have to learn to breath through his mouth, and much care had to be taken so he would not choke or get food down his windpipe. After taking very small amounts of nourishment, the process became a little more acceptable, especially when there was no other alternative.

He was nurtured slowly back to health. After a year and four months, he was finally released from the US Hospital in Paris, and after much celebrating by the staff and the joys and heartbreaks of goodbyes, he was taken on board a Hospital Ship and returned to the United States. He was given a discharge from the Army shortly thereafter, and returned to Minnesota, in June 1920.

Because of his extensive damage to the inside of his mouth, and loss of so many teeth, he sought and received Government Paid dental care. He chose to work with Doctor W.H. McGonagle, in Royalton, Minnesota. Between the good dentist and my father's good patience, they were able to reconstruct his bite. For many years, Doctor McGonagle's dedication to his profession and his patients, especially my dad, earned him great respect in the community. The government paid for the gold that replaced my father's teeth that were shot out, but the skill of shaping the gold so my father could chew his food, was credited to the good dentist. I have always felt that just being here, alive, on this earth was miraculous, and when one considers "if that hot machine gun bullet that hit my dad, had entered an inch in any direction different than it did, I would not be here doing what I am doing!"

My dad liked horses. One day he found out about a trainload of wild mustangs being brought into Royalton. He was one of the first to bring home a couple of wild horses. They were rounded up in Wyoming, Colorado or one of the western states. Once he got them to the farm, by trailer, he would patiently and kindly make friends with them. Eventually getting their confidence enough, to work alongside one of the big horses in the field. Dad always said, "a horse is a curious animal, but they by nature are more apt to flee when sensing confrontation." In order to get them to come to him, dad would take a pail with some oats, and hiding the halter, would tempt the curious wild horse, pet it's head, talk gently to it, give it some hands full of oats, and then when the horse was relaxed, he'd slip the halter on. On giving advice about horses, dad said "it is best to walk just a little behind the head of the horse, making believe that the animal is leading you, while you steer it where you want it to go." He was also an advocate of treating the horse with kindness and to never raise your voice to them, for they are excitable and any harshness raises their heartbeat by twenty beats per minute.

We had a pair of draft horses on the farm, Belgians. Their names were Denver and Powder. The names were picked because when my dad was a young teenager, he spent time in the Powder River Basin in Wyoming as a ranch hand. It was there, where he learned so many things about one of man's most valuable animals, the horse. On his way home several years later, he went to Denver, where he caught the train back eventually to Minnesota. These names were special to him. Several years later, we acquired two more big horses, and they were named Chubby and Bobby. They were a great team. My dad went to the Harnessmaker in Buckman, Minnesota, to have new harnesses made to fit them. The Harnessmaker had to come to the farm to measure up those horses.

My dad and I would stop at the Shop from time to time to see the progress of the tailor made new harnesses. You'd never forget the smell of a Harnessmakers Shop. There's nothing else like it in the world. It was wonderful, the smell of tanned, oiled leather. The big sewing machine was German made. The spools of thread were Cream, Red, Black, Blue, and Green. The spools were cone shaped, and the fiber was very strong. The different colors that were used depended upon the part of the harness that was being sewn.

When they were finally finished, the Harnessmaker delivered them, and they fit to a tee!

Nothing came close to the talent and ability of that patient man. He was uncompromising.

Yet had such an easy disposition. Years later, as I no longer remember his name; I do recall the words of tribute I dedicated to him. "When a great man dies, we look all around for another to take his place. But none comes. And none will. His class is extinguished, and him with it. In another trade - In another time, the next great man will appear." The gifted Harnessmaker's contribution to society went far beyond tanning, oiling, cutting and sewing leather. His talent helped settle our great country, because "he was able to harness the energy and strength of the horses", and made it possible to improve our world.

An early blizzard in the fall of 1938 blew snowdrifts over six feet high near the end of our driveway. The road past our farm was noted for getting drifted shut. The high drifts would obscure the dirt country road. Passers by would often end up in the ditch because the high drifts made it impossible to see where the road was. That stormy afternoon, a neighbor came to our house and asked if my dad could pull him out with the tractor.

That old tractor hadn't been started in over a month, and the oil was thicker than molasses. Besides that, it was almost completely covered by a snowdrift. My dad said that the tractor would never start, but he would harness up one of the horses, and pull the car out of the ditch for him. The man laughed and said, “a horse would never pull that car out!” My dad just went ahead and took the big horse out of the barn to where the car was buried in the snow filled ditch. They had to shovel out a place in front of the car in order to hook up the log chain to the car. With the chain hooked to the car and the horse, my dad took the reins and said to the patient, gentle horse: “Giddup”. To the amazement of the skeptic, his car seemed to pop right out of the ditch. I looked on in my own disbelief, at how strong and powerful the horse really is!

Chapter Four: Little Pig Market

I spent a lot of time with my dad, and was learning to "read him", and what he wanted to do next. It seemed to me I could almost anticipate what he needed me to do to help. We had become "working partners". The year was 1939. My dad and I had just finished loading up the two wheeled trailer with newly weaned little pigs. They were all clean, cute and playful with one another as we put the tailgate on the trailer. "Well, we'd better get started." Getting the little pigs to the market early usually brought the best prices. My dad and I got into our '33 Chevrolet sedan and left the farm for Little Falls, and "The Biggest Little Pig Market in the World".

My dad drove carefully as we headed down the gravel road to the State Road. After a few miles, we were on the Blacktop Highway. My dad took me along with him most everywhere he went. I thought it was because he liked my company! But I really knew it was so he could keep an eye on me.

On our journey, we went through the Village of Buckman, on to Genola, and almost to Pierz, turning west on Highway 27, toward Little Falls, Minnesota.

"Charles Lindburgh rode his motorcycle on this road a few years back", my dad said. He pointed out the farms along the way, all groomed to perfection and noted that most all the farmers around the area were German. "Most of them still spoke

German. They came here to Morrison County because of the opportunities that were so plentiful in the area." Because of the good thick, rich soil, abundant rainfall for the crops and good grass for livestock, "most of these farmers were well to do, and you can see by the way they keep their farms looking like a garden."

We didn't know what was in store for us in the years to come, but we were aware that Germany, under Adolf Hitler, was building up it's military power and building advanced aircraft. Germany was already taking advantage of its neighboring European countries.

When we arrived in Little Falls, we headed straight for Market Street. There we saw dozens of trailer loads and pickup beds of little pigs parked along the street. The "Buyers" would come by with a pointer stick in one hand and poke around a little at the piggies to make sure they were all healthy. The Buyer would then make an offer. It was like "15 cents" or "17 cents" or maybe "18 cents" if the little pigs looked exceptionally good. My dad tried to hold out for 18 cents, but it looked like the offer we had for 17 cents was top for us.

The Buyers were making offers for "Live Weight".

Another Buyer came by again and said "17 cents", and my dad said, "OK". We then drove the car and trailer around to a large scale where we were weighed, (car, trailer and all), and given a little white slip of paper. Then we had to unload the little fellas into crates and drive the car and trailer around to the scale a second time to get another white slip. The Buyer took the two slips, did some figuring, and just pulled out a pocket full of paper money and paid my dad in cash on the spot. If my memory serves me right, it was about $66.00 for fourteen little pigs.

After that, we got back in the car with an empty trailer behind and started for home. We were without much to say for a few miles, but I finally wanted to know, "what happens to these little pigs after today?" Then dad told me, "Oh, they get treated very well. Get plenty to eat, and well cared for until they get big. After that, they will be butchered for hams, bacon, loin roasts, pork chops, side pork and sausages.

Whatever is left over will go to fertilizer."

I couldn't help thinking about the final fate of these little piggies and as we drove, I looked at my dad and he looked a little remorseful, too.

At Genola, we stopped for ice cream cones.

A month or so later, in the summer of 1939, I was five years and five months old, and eager to explore more and more of the world around me. Across the road from our driveway was a small swamp or wetland. A lot of birds made nests in the protection of that collected water. Nature was abundant in that area. There were "cat-tails", "pussy willows", "cow slip" flowers that bloomed with pretty yellow flowers and sat on top of the water. They seemed to always be just beyond reach, and it would be dangerous to try to pick them, for falling in the water.

Alongside the road, were wild strawberries. They are a little hard to find until you know where to look for them. Wild strawberries are wonderful. They grow about as big as a raspberry, but the taste is wonderfully unique and beyond delicious description! I liked taking a little woven cane basket with a soft cloth inside that my mother would give me to put the little berries in as I found and picked them. I would pick as many as I could to try to fill the little basket. When I picked a basket full of the perfectly ripened berries, I would take them back to the house where my mom would clean off the stems, (and a bug or two, once in a while), and carefully wash them. After our evening meal, I sat proudly and watched my mother serve everybody a tiny bowl of wild strawberries with a dollop of freshly made sweet whipping cream on top. The little dessert was a great way to finish dinner.

On September 1st, 1939, the German Army invaded Poland, and that aggressive act was the start of World War Two.

It was also the first day of school, but I was only five and a half years old. Nevertheless, my parents made arrangements with the Teacher, Mrs. Begordis, for me to go to school "to visit". I wanted to go to school and I was more than ready! Because I had older brothers, it was easy for me to pick up on all kinds of knowledge. When my older brothers came home from school, my parents always asked, "What did you learn in school today?" Then I would hear the recap of my brothers telling my parents about what they learned every day.

I had already learned to read, write, draw, knew geography, could read world maps and recite, but could not enter the first grade at District 115 in central Morrison County. I begged to visit school more and more often, until one day the teacher finally had to tell my parents, "He just can't 'visit' at school anymore." My parents were disappointed by the teachers' decision, but understood why. I was heartbroken. By her announcement, she went on to say, "this little boy is already further along than my third and fourth graders, and he just cannot keep coming to school (to visit) anymore!"

Having to stay home for another full year was not a very good thing for me. I spent so much time with my dad, and when I was in the house, I read Mother Goose stories and Nursery Rhymes, along with books my older brother brought from school.

Chapter Five: The War Years

As the German Army advanced through Poland and into the Ukraine, I began following the News Reports on the Radio, very closely. I would get up early in the morning in order to hear the six o'clock news. I remember hearing all the correspondents giving their reports from many different cities in the world, especially London, Paris and Berlin. They all reported details of how the war was going, and the battles that were being (mostly) lost. It was not long after the war started, that the reports were no longer broadcast from Berlin.

The Germans were capturing city after city like falling domino's in Eastern Europe. Adolf Hitler gloated in the Third Reich's early victories, and in his arrogance, supported by the largest, best trained, and well equipped soldiers, defied world opinion and plunged headlong into furthering his conquests.

The time was very successful for the Nazi's. After easy victories in Poland, Germany went into France, and pushed the English Army off the continent. Times looked dark and bleak for the Allies. The German army occupied Paris, as the French Army surrendered, being no match for the highly mechanized Germans. The French resistance easily broke down, and the country of France submitted to a German sponsored government.

In 1940, the people of the United States were still strongly divided and opposed the war. Many, many people were not willing to commit the young men in America to fight and die in a war "not of our own making!" However, the United States was sending strategic supplies to England from the very beginning of hostilities.

The German Luftwaffe ruled the skies throughout Europe, except for England. Added to that, German V-1 rockets targeted London, causing heavy damage.

School started in the fall of 1940, and I had lost much of my intensity and zeal. My desire to enter first grade, was awakened by a new young teacher, Miss Hegg. She was bright, and took charge. She played with the students at recess when her time permitted. I found myself more interested in what was being taught in the one room schoolhouse to the fourth graders, however. I was not interested in "seeing Dick and Jane" or "watching Spot run and jump", anymore. Miss Hegg was our teacher for the years 1940 – 41 and 1941 – 42. She did a respectable job.

In the fall of 1940, my dad bought a new Chevrolet Special Deluxe for $850.00. It was dark green, a wonderful automobile. It rode and drove like a million! The last lingering effects of the Stock Market Crash of 1929 and results of the Great Depression that followed were still prevalent. These deep influencing factors caused caution to reign and doubts to trouble the financial world as World War Two loomed ever closer for America's involvement. Throughout occupied Europe, the Nazi's were rounding up Jewish People and others disloyal to The Party, sending them off to Labor and Concentration Camps. Their lives being torn apart, families being separated, and never to be heard from again. Never knowing the eventual fate of loved ones, if they may have lived or died. And most died.

In December, 1941, the Imperial Navy of Japan bombed Pearl Harbor. We listened all day to the reports coming in of sunken ships, and loss of life. The United States formally declared war on Japan on December 7th, and the following day, December 8th, declared war on Germany. The full intensity and passionate struggles were just beginning for the people of the United States. For the Allies, was the despair of many more dark days yet to come.

Winter is the season of most inconveniences. During the winter of '41 – '42, as a young, seven year old, I had chores to do every day after school and into the night. Schoolwork was something that just had to wait. It was done right before bedtime by kerosene lamp on the kitchen table. In our home in the winter, we always had a wood burning, stove for cooking. Our house did not have a furnace, but rather, what was called an "Airtight Heater". It was in the center of the main room of the house. It would be fired up to its maximum capacity just before going to bed in order to get as much heat in the house as possible on severely cold winter nights. As kids, we had mounds and mounds of blankets on our beds. Seeing our breath in the morning was as common as seeing snow outside. One of my jobs was to carry wood into the house and fill the “woodbox”. Every day I would fill the woodbox to capacity.

We became so used to working and getting chores done each day, we didn’t realize we were “just children”, while we did the work. We never even questioned it! Life on the farm, especially in the wintertime, was a difficult time, and a lot of hard work. Every morning, I would jump out of bed, and get clothes on so I could go downstairs, get warm, and listen to the News Reports about how the war was going. Both Germany and Japan were scoring sizeable victories in the European and Pacific Theatres of war. The Japanese took over the Phillipine Islands, and the Germans were gaining strangleholds on the Russian cities of Moscow, Leningrad, and Stalingrad.

Many German soldiers were able to spend their Christmas "at Home" in 1941, as a reward, attending parties in celebration of their heroic victories. There was much drinking, singing, and dancing at the seasons "Fausching Celebrations" in the large and small cities alike.

Back on the farm in Minnesota, one spring day, a truck pulled into our yard. An old gentleman got out of the passenger side and asked if we had any junk field equipment, cast iron, or other metal we wanted to sell. The year was 1942, and as a matter of fact, we had a bunch of old scrap iron to get rid of. The old man saw a lot more than we realized lying around the farmyard, rusting. As he surveyed and picked out pieces to load on the truck, he would ask my dad; "this too?", and with my dad's consent, the item would be loaded on the truck. The Wilinsky Brothers were dealers in scrap iron and metals from Minneapolis. It was a wise decision for them to canvass the countryside for old farm machinery. For what was estimated to be one thousand pounds of scrap iron and metal, the old man handed my dad twelve dollars in brand new crisp currency. They then went on their way to the next neighbor and the next, and so on. In the end, we heard they filled a railroad car, which they had reserved in Royalton. All this, of course, was to provide materials to the smelters for war production. It was also an opportunity for the farmers to clean up their farmyards, make a few extra dollars, as well as contributing to the war effort.

Those were the days of Government War Rationing. The Federal Government was quick to set regulations to strictly limit certain items which might be hoarded. We had little tokens for this, and little tabs for that. Stamps and certificates for other things. What I best remember on the tight rationing list were butter, sugar, tires, inner tubes, and gasoline. They were strictly controlled. The joke was, "If you had bad tires when the war started, they would probably be a lot worse by the time the war finally ended!" The speed limit for passenger cars was thirty-five miles per hour, and was strictly obeyed by every good citizen. The factories that had been turning out products for civilian consumption were quickly turned into defense plants.

The War Department had extremely powerful means to implement the changes in both large and small businesses to convert to wartime manufacturing, and during that time, everybody contributed and gave their best efforts.

Our family bought War Bonds when we had the money, and war stamps were sold in the schools, and by the local stores, as well as the mailman and the Post Office. The war stamps were smaller than a postage stamp, and came in different colors identifying the denominations of values. Green were ten cents; blue, twenty-five cents; red, fifty cents, if my memory serves me correct. When the booklet was full, all the entries added up to eighteen dollars and fifty cents. At that point, the book would be traded in for a War Bond.

As an eight year old, I planted a "Victory Garden", as we were encouraged to do. I took care of preparing the ground, tilling, raking, planting in rows and the weeding hoeing and harvesting of its produce. My victory garden was next to the family garden, which was tended to by both my dad and mother.

The Rural Free Delivery mailman, Bargabos, sold us most of the War Bonds and War Stamps, if you met him at the mailbox. We sent Mail Orders off regularly to Sears, Roebuck, and Montgomery Ward for many of the necessities that we needed. With Tires and Gasoline both being tightly rationed, the convenience of Mail Orders became increasingly popular as well as economical and prudent.

On our farm, we had about 48 milking cows. It was demanding work, but also rewarding. My dad was very particular about the cleanliness of the milk cows, the pails we used, and the milk cans. The temperature was also a very important issue, especially in the summer.

My father would pump all the stock tanks full with fresh cold water every day. As soon as milking was done, the milk cans were promptly placed into the cold water of one of the tanks to allow the milk to cool down, and be ready for the "milk hauler" to pick up every following morning. In later years, the local creamery began "sanitizing" the milk cans with a high temperature "steam process". It reduced the possibility of bacteria greatly.

As I became old enough, I was expected to do more of the hard work. School started in the fall of 1942, and we were lucky to have a bright and dedicated new teacher that replaced Miss Hegg. Our new teacher was from the rural community of Grey Eagle, Minnesota, and her name was Ruth Kaiser.

She was the best teacher I would have from grades one to six. She was organized, and skilled in her ability to bring out the best in her students. She made the learning process fun and created enthusiasm in us, which propelled our energy and desire to please her.

Each day after school, one of my jobs was to go up into the silo, and chop frozen silage away from the walls of the silo. It had to be done right after school, early enough in the evening in order to have daylight to see. The silo was 28 feet high, and each night, I would climb up the rungs to the level where I had to work. I had to use a tool called a "silage chopper". It had a long handle, and was heavy enough to break the frozen chopped cornstalks up, so they could be thrown down the silo chute, and then given to the cows, until all of them were fed. It was hard back-breaking work. As I broke the chunks loose, and threw them down, my older brother, Erv, would take them from the base of the chute, to the mangers of each one of the milk cows until they were all fed. It was cold, and work was sometimes almost futile. I remember always yelling down to Erv, "is it almost enough?"

His answer would be "No, I still have eight more to feed", or something like that. I could hardly wait to climb back down from the inside of that cold silo each night. My body would be so cold, especially my hands and feet. It seemed like it took forever to get warmed up again.

As the year 1942 ended, and '43 began, we realized the desperate struggles that were taking place in the war. It was do or die, for both the

Allied and Axis powers. The British and American Armies finally defeated the Germans in North Africa, a major morale builder. With the Germans retreating to Italy, the Allies gained a little room to plan coming assaults.

On the eastern front, three major cities were still under siege, but the German Army was unable to capture and claim them. The Russians began receiving "Lend-lease Aid" from the United States. Furious battles were fought in Russia, and as an early winter set in, the German Troops were caught, unprepared for the cold, and lost momentum. Many froze to death. By the end of 1943, over three million German Soldiers had been killed, wounded or taken prisoner.

The hour had turned bleak for Hitler, and many Germans knew that they could no longer win the war. Adolf Hitler might have well taken a history lesson from Napoleon.

The United States Army's Eighth Airforce and English Airforce began making routine bombing runs over mainland Europe into Germany. The cost was high, with many of the bombers, B 17's, B 24's and English Lancasters, being shot down, mainly by flak from ground Anti-aircraft-artillery and aggressive 109 Messerschmitts.

By the end of May, 1943, our school became aware that Miss Kaiser would not be returning to teach at District 115, in Buckman Township, Morrison County. With a tear in our eyes, we wished the best for her on her new assignment.

In 1944, at the age of ten, I was interested as ever in the events of the war. America started seeing better results in the Pacific. The war with the Japanese was more of an all out effort on the part of the United States, as opposed to Europe.

The Russians were taking a huge brunt of the fighting in the east. Casualties were heavy on both sides. Allied forces were bogged down in Italy, but the trend was slowly shifting in favor of the Allies. On June 6th, 1944, the Allied forces stormed the French Coast, and D-Day had begun. The Russians were headed toward Budapest, where the Germans were determined to hold the city at all costs. They did not.

In December, American forces were engaged in the Battle of the Bulge, where the Germans threw everything they had and put on a strong offensive in early winter, but after fierce fighting, and heavy casualties, end results for the Germans were diminished and the German Army was never able to mount a sustained effort again. Losses for the Americans were our heaviest in the war around Bastogne, Belgium, where it was under siege.

In the Pacific, there were Australian, British, Canadian, and New Zealanders fighting with

America, however, the main responsibility was with the fighting men of the United States against the Japanese in the Pacific Theatre. American warplanes began bombing the cities of Japan, including Tokyo, taking hostilities to their front door.

School had just let out at 3:30 in the afternoon, as I jumped off the steps of the District 115 schoolhouse. On a normal day, I would have run the mile and a quarter from school to home. Before I could even think about it, I saw my Uncle Phillip in the car waiting to give us a ride home. Phillip had two sons and a daughter, he was picking up, and he told my two brothers and me to get in the car to ride along. It was not unusual that he did this, especially in the wintertime. There was some blowing and drifting snow, but not a bad storm. "Tomorrow will be my tenth birthday", I thought to myself as we rode in the car. Then, as Uncle Phillip approached our driveway, he drove right on by, instead of dropping us off as he usually did. I could see a strange car in our yard next to the house, and wondered, "what's going on?" For some reason I had a feeling something was wrong with my mother. My intuition was nearly correct, but there was no explanation for us having to stay overnight at Phillip and Mary's. We just sometimes did that. After nightfall, and before bedtime, I noticed Aunt Mary praying the Rosary. I knew she was praying for my mother, without a doubt. I knew as well, that Aunt Mary had not gone to church for many years, but for this night, the light of her faith was alive and aglow. I felt fear for my mother again at that moment, and the thought roused unanswered questions anew in my mind. "What is going on?"

Later, as we got ready for bed, she took my hand and said, "tomorrow everything will be alright, I promise." From that night on, I held a very special place in my heart for Aunt Mary. I fell fast asleep, and the next thing I knew as I awoke, "I was ten years old!" Uncle Phillip drove us all off to school without anyone knowing it was my birthday.

At the end of the school day, I couldn't wait to get home. I was curious as could be as to what happened at our house. When I came in the door of our house, I saw my mother holding a little baby boy. My parents had already decided to name him Darwin.

He was a pretty special addition to our family, especially when you consider, living on a farm is just not always that exciting. Soon after, I started helping take care of the baby, and for some reason . . . . . I became more settled. I was less intense, not quite so deliberate. Not running full speed everywhere I went as much, more satisfied with the moment.

This little baby began to help me find a new feeling of fulfillment. I was making myself useful to my mother. She showed me her appreciation for being interested and being helpful in many little ways.

It was over five years since my mother and dad formed the pact, agreeing that I had to be with my dad wherever he went. I had grown so very accustomed to him. I knew just what he would do next, because I had learned to read his actions and almost his mind.

As I had for the past five years, spent so much time with my dad, I hardly realized how I had emotionally withdrawn from mother. Now, once again, we seemed to be rebuilding a closer relationship, and it felt good. What we had begun to restore was the most unforgettable birthday present my mother ever gave me. The restoring of her love and trust in me.

She had re-discovered the little boy in me.

Winter eased into spring, and the war seemed to be going somewhat better, although, the Germans and the Japanese were very formidable enemies. It was 1944, and we were all working harder than ever on the farm. We had our own farm of 80 acres, plus the vacant Kranz farm just east, and the vacant farm next to ours to the south, with 120 and 80 acres, gave us more land than we had ever farmed before. In addition to that was the 20 acres dad rented from Uncle Tony, with about 6 acres under the plow.

Dad was trying to get petitions signed in order to keep Donald on the farm. The draft board passed Donald over for the month of June, 1944. Dad was successful in getting an extension of his deferment for six months, due to the heavy workload on the farm.

The local draft board was calling up eighteen year olds as soon as they had birthdays. Donald would be nineteen in August. With the workload as heavy as it was, dad ordered a new tractor over a year earlier, but because it was wartime, all the factories and assembly plants were turning out military equipment. Finally, a big new red Farmall was shipped to the Implement Dealer, partially assembled! The big tractor tires were shipped from one place, and the fuel tank from another, the engine, still another place. Seeing it the first time, it looked like a big wounded bird. All the parts were finally received, (scavenged from all over). The Mischke Implement Dealer in Buckman did the final work and the tractor was delivered in May of 1944. What a wonderful tractor it was. Solid, big and powerful.

Through the summer, everyone in the family worked, and we were all rewarded for our efforts and attitudes. Often, dad would make a deal with us boys; "if you get the chores done early enough, we'll go to the show tonight!" The movie theatre was about 12 miles away in Pierz, called the "Star Theatre". I can still see the marquee, and little white lights that chased around adding a magical touch to the experience. And the Popcorn, the aroma, I can still smell it as we entered into the carpeted lobby.

Before the main feature, there was always the “Movietone News, showing gruesome footage of recently fought battles of the war. Fear grew in the hearts of many mothers for their sons who were called on to fight in that terrible and bloody, six year carnage.

The main feature was always preceded by a cartoon, then a Gene Autry or Roy Rogers cowboy show. Even they had their roles to play in those stressful, tense times. If only for a few hours, it took us away from the harsh reality of a war that raged on.

Many religious preachers took advantage of “earthquakes, floods, volcanic eruptions, rumors of wars, and war”, to dupe the people, predicting the end of the world. Many people believed in the prophesies of the bible that "armageddon" had finally arrived. But as the announced days came, the world survived, the earth kept turning, and the brutal fighting of the terrible war, continued.

On a Sunday afternoon toward the end of summer, I took the .410 gage shotgun (with my dad's permission) out into the woods northwest of our farm. My dad approved because he knew I was very careful and spent time with the gun under his supervision.

It was a great experience for me to walk in the woods under the canopy of the trees and to hear, see and enjoy the different little birds and animals that lived there. When nature is left unto itself, it does its own governing.

As I walked through the tall red oak woods, I came across a large gray hornets hive hanging from one of the branches. Hornets are unpredictable, and tend to get after horses if they get excited. Most farmers dread the sight of a hornet around a horse.

I couldn't reach the hive, but I found a stick long enough to "bat it down". I could see no activity around the nest, which was as large as a coffee pot. Without thinking any further, I walked up to the cone shaped hive and took a swipe at it with the stick. The hive was attached better than I expected, and did not fall, but the damage stirred up a whole bunch of hornets that didn't think much of my intentions. Without a moments pause, I turned, picked up the little shotgun, and ran for home as fast as I could. As I ran, I was swatting and getting stung at least a half dozen times. One of the stings was near my right eye, others on my arms, hands and neck. These hornets have a very hard sting!

I ran all the way back to the farmyard and right into the house, grabbed a couple of shotgun shells and the .12 gage shotgun (long tom, we called it), and went right back out into the woods again! As I approached the damaged hive, there was still some activity, and I was concerned about getting stung again. So I inched up ever closer and raised the gun to line up the sight. The large shell was loaded with #10 buckshot in the chamber as I cocked the hammer back and squeezed the trigger.

Blamm . . . . !
The recoil set me back abruptly on my butt, as I gathered myself together, I quickly looked and saw the blast had blown the nest to smithereens! There was hardly a trace of hornets left. With a bruised shoulder and the beestings, I felt like I had just returned from some kind of war zone. My dad was not pleased about my adventure with the hornets and let it be known to me. He said, "from now on, get permission ahead of time to use the .12 gage!"

The end of summer meant harvest time and back to school, again. As the harvest started, we all managed to help out and worked with the neighbors back and forth. I started driving the new tractor off and on and it was a great experience. I had some difficulty with pushing in the clutch pedal all the way down, but found if I stood up, and braced against the seat, I could do it every time. The tractor was a beautiful cherry red and a magnificent machine! It had five forward gears and one reverse. Fifth gear was "road gear", and the top speed was about 21 miles per hour! The tractor was equipped with two bright headlights, hydraulics for power lifts, and power takeoff. After I learned to drive it, I would ask my dad if I could park it in the car shed. The car sat out most of the time anyway, so I would dutifully start the tractor every evening and drive it into the car shed. If it rained, it wouldn't be all wet the next morning.

With so many young men in uniform, there was an acute shortage of workers for agriculture. As the grain was cut and threshed, the granary was filled, the haybarn was filled with hay for winter, and the silo was filled with chopped cornstalks for silage. Any accesses were hauled, and sold to the grain elevator in Genola. Then, we braced for another winter.

Chapter Six: Goodbye, My Friend

November 1944, was the last Thanksgiving we would all spend together as a family. Due to a blizzard, we ended up with some soldiers at our house who were on their way home. The storm was so bad, they just couldn't travel any further than our farm. My mother just set two more places, and we enjoyed having them at our table. Both if them had life threatening experiences. One was shot and lost his right lung but was grateful to be alive and almost home. The other young man was rescued out of the cold north Atlantic after their ship was torpedoed. He was not as willing to describe his experience, but was thankful for the good food and warm hospitality.

December 1st, Donald received his induction notice from the local draft board in Little Falls, instructing him to report to the Federal Building in Minneapolis, February 3rd, 1945.

Donald was my bed partner from almost as early as I can remember. He would let me put my cold feet on his back to try to stay warm in the upstairs of that cold house. He held me close to his body on cold winter nights, or I surly would have frozen to death. He was nineteen, and I was ten. I felt fortunate for the few extra months he was able to remain at home. On the day he left for the Army, I tried to say "goodbye", (a word I never really learned), and took one last look at him as I went off to school, and shut the door behind me.

"God, how I hated to see him have to leave!"

As soon as I found out his training camp address, I wrote him letters. By April 20th, the war with Germany was over. We relaxed some as the fighting ceased and Germany succumbed to an unconditional surrender. It didn't take long for the reports to start coming back to the States of the horrible findings and gruesome conditions that were discovered in the camps where prisoners and any detainees had been held. The fate of those who were still alive in the camps left the rescuers in absolute disbelief.

Airmen from bombers that were shot down along with allied soldiers and servicemen from all branches of the military were herded into prison camps. Those who didn't die lived in the horrible stench among the dead.

All traces of hope had been abandoned by most of the prisoners. Because of the long duration of the war, the German people themselves were facing starvation. There was but little agriculture left in the collapsing infrastructure.

The officials were first in line for what food that was available, next German military, then the privileged citizens, and finally the less fortunate citizens. Any undesirables and prisoners were beyond sustenance. Those who were alive were found to be nothing but skeletons. Due to the scarcity of food, the humans in the concentration camps were the last to be appropriated food. Because they were the enemies of the "state", it would seem starvation would be "fair punishment" in the eyes of the captors. Most of Europe was on the verge of starvation as the war ended and only massive food distribution programs saved an even greater catastrophe.

The Japanese were defending their remaining held islands in the Pacific with every fiber of resistance they could muster. Both the Americans and Japanese took on very heavy casualties as the United States captured island after island on the way to Japan proper.

The gasoline gelatin flamethrower was introduced late in the war in order to drive the enemy out of their defensive positions they occupied in the mountain caves. Most of the Japanese refused to surrender, so they were "burned out" of their positions. The fear of "dishonor" to the Emperor kept the Japanese Army disciplined to the end. It was just plain ugly!

Because of my high level of personal interest in the current events of World War Two, I got up early every morning, to track the historical progress of the war. I listened eagerly to the reports of correspondents from their respective locations in the world. If there would be a new unfamiliar city or country mentioned or reported from, I would look up its location on the maps, which our family had in an encyclopedia, or various resources we had in our home. I listened mostly to CBS because it was the most powerful station available in our area of central Minnesota. As a young boy, my quest for information was "insatiable". As history unfolded day by day, through the course of the war, I cataloged these events and my memory of this very desperate struggle, remains.

For over six long years in the most formative years of my life, I was exposed to the desperation of what it means "to be at war".

All of this, because of failure of leaders of countries and ignorance of politicians, lack of ability or desire to find common ground and talk to one another.

Taking the young men, who have not yet tasted life's nectar and using them as pawns, to please the whims of arrogant, self serving, leaders, is wrong!!

To kill or be killed . . . . . . .there is no Glory in war !

I saw too many young men come home in coffins, and heard of too many men missing in action. And I knew too many men who were too shot up to be able to live a reasonable life because their life was spared!

Many of our neighbors' sons, and my uncles, and cousins lost their lives. They found it necessary to lie in muddy, wet and contemptible foxholes, with only hope that tomorrow would still spare their lives, if fate allowed.

To the kin of lost soldiers; mothers, fathers, sisters, brothers, wives, children and loved ones, the piercing pain of grief for a lifetime, remains. Where is the dignity of mankind, when one man must go out to shoot and kill another whom he has never met? Having perchance, met the other person, who knows, they might like each other! Yet, they must engage one another without the knowledge of who each other are.

After induction into the Army, Donald was sent to Camp Wolters, Texas. The army camp was near Mineral Wells, just west of Fort Worth. I wrote him a letter every day, "just so that he would always get mail!" Mother wrote often too, and he answered as his time allowed.

Farm work was an extra burden on us in the spring and summer of 1945. I was now eleven years old, and drove tractor extensively to keep the field crops healthy. Cutting and raking hay, cultivating corn, pulling the grain binder, hauling double grain wagons, were all in a days work. My older brother, Erv, pumped water for the livestock, worked with the big horses, and helped my dad more with the farm chores, feeding pigs, and making sure the animals were well tended to.

My uncle Phillip drove into our farmyard one summer day, and told my dad; "I saw your new tractor going across the field as I was comin' down the road, and it looked like nobody was on it!" Dad said, "Oh, there's somebody on it alright, but he's pretty small, and kinda hard to see from the road!" Uncle Phillip laughed about that for the rest of the summer!.

My uncle George needed some help, so my dad and I went out east to Lakin Township, and I ended up staying for nine or ten days. While I was there, for one thing, we dug and harvested rutabega's, lots of them. Picked fresh sweet corn, and dug a few potatoes, and took the ripe tomatoes off the vines every day.

While I was there, every day at noon, my aunt Annie called us for lunch. On our way in from the fields, uncle George and I would wash up at the water pump. Then he would pull out his beer bottle opener, and snap open two bottles of beer. Uncle George always had Grain Belt Premium Beer that he kept in a "cold box" near the well. Then as he handed me a cold bottle of beer, he said every day, "If you have to work like a man, you can drink like a man!" It was the best tasting beer I ever had in my life. Uncle George always bought beer in brown bottles, by the case, because he said the minute the sun shines on a clear bottle, it makes the beer taste "skunky!" He would know!

The 13th of August, Donald had his 20th birthday. He was scheduled to come home on leave within the next few weeks or so for seven or ten days. On the farm, we were all excited.

There just isn't that much excitement on the farm.

I wanted to make sure everything was in "tip-top" shape when he came home on furlough. The grain in the fields was looking the best we had ever seen it. The many fields of corn were freshly cultivated and growing so high the tassels touched the top frame of the cultivators on the new big tractor. In my spare time, I washed and polished Donald's car. He had a 1931 Chevrolet four door sedan that waited for him when he got home. Dad said it was okay for me to start it up and drive it around the farmyard a little to keep the battery charged up full. I sent a mail order to Montgomery Ward for a can of White Sidewall Tire Paint, and carefully painted on white sidewalls.

I found two long thin strips of chrome of equal length, and put them on the front radiator in the form of a "V for Victory". Did his car ever look sharp, all shiny black and clean, with light green spoke wheels and whitewall tires!

The following day, the United States dropped the first atom bomb on the Japanese city of Hiroshima, killing thousands of civilians. The event was so traumatic that there was wide spread speculation that the war in the Pacific would be over in the next few days. However, about a week passed and a second bomb was dropped on Nagasaki, with equal or greater devastation. A few days later, the Japanese surrendered on the Battleship Missouri to General Douglas McArthur. September 1st, the signing took place in Tokyo Bay, with the Emperor placing his signature on the documents.

The whole country broke out into festivities, hereto unprecedented. The radio news broadcasts were jubilant. The music was playing, "When the Lights Go on Again All Over the World", and "There'll be Bluebirds Over the White Cliffs of Dover, Tomorrow When the World is Free". How happy we all were! At long last! The whole nation was caught up in frenzied celebrations.

Peace, peace, peace, at last !

We had won the War and there is peace at Last !

The days passed rather quickly, with the end of the war and all. It was going on the 3rd of September, and my mother paced worriedly around all day. "If only he'd write!" There was no letter again today. I knew she was feeling great pain, but there wasn't a thing anyone in the family could do to help. It seemed as though days had passed since we last heard from Donald. It visibly affected mother and she was deeply troubled. I heard her say again, "If only he'd write, even just a few lines, to let us know he's alright!"

The newscasts were jubilant over the ending of the war, and yet, we were feeling some kind of deep pain. "Why doesn't he write?"

Then came Saturday night. At about 9:45 on the 4th of September, my brothers and I were already upstairs in bed, when we heard a car drive into our yard, and a knock on the door. The door was answered and we could hear several voices speaking in low tones. We couldn't hear what was being said, but whoever the late evening visitors were, spoke quietly, and there were pauses, and more low tones of the visitors voices and again pauses.

Whoever they were, they left after about an hour. As they left the farmyard, we fell asleep, unaware of the news they had brought.

I got up early the next morning as I always did, and took our cattle dog, "Rex", out in the pasture to get the cows in for the morning milking. My brother, Erv, (14 years old) and I were almost half done milking about 44 cows, when we began to realize dad had not yet come out to the barn, which was very unusual. Minutes later, I was bringing a full pail of milk to the cream separator, and saw my mother standing just inside the door. She looked like a Ghost! I thought she was dreadfully ill. I asked, "What's wrong . . . . .?" and she told me, "Donald drowned."

We had to help each other to get back to the house. Sobbing uncontrollably, she could find no place of comfort from her broken heart and her pain within. I hardly remember going back to help Erv finish the milking. Dad was too grief stricken to even come out to help. The drowning took place on September 2nd, the day after the war ended, at a place called "Possum

Kingdom" in Camp Wolters, Texas. Little did we know how our lives would change and become affected by this tragedy. Words simply fall short.

Such a disappointment! There is nothing more that can be said.

It seemed like a large stone was in my stomach, and it would not go away. We had the days ahead to try to find strength to get through. I prayed.

It was every bit as much as we could bear. The body was shipped from Texas to Royalton, Minnesota on the train. The weather was unusually hot, and the escorts were concerned that the body would begin breaking down before it arrived at it's destination. In order to salvage the embalmed body, a glass cover was fitted into the casket to allow the family and friends to view this soldier one last time.

The funeral and burial was hastily planned. The escorts made sure no time was lost as they pressed the arrangements. There would be only one night for the many people who knew him and of him. Early the next morning, only our immediate family took one last look at the body and the casket was closed. A long procession of cars followed down the state road to Morrill, where Donald would be laid to rest next to his maternal grandmother.

After the funeral services, the casket was taken to the cemetery and placed over the open freshly prepared grave. The Honor Guard took the

Red, White, and Blue flag from the casket, and crisply folded it and handed it to my mother, as they fired a 21 gun salute in his last honor. Finally, a lone trumpeter, labored through the sorrowful taps that must have settled into every field and meadow around the countryside: The final tribute, to this young man.

I tried to keep composed. For the first time during the stressful event, I turned around and saw how many people had attended this funeral. The whole community was truly grief stricken. People came from all around. There were estimates that over 500 people had come to help us share our loss. It was a very hot day, and most of the people had to endure the heat outside, because there was only room for about 100 people in the church.

Many of them came to our farm after the funeral. They brought with them, food, and their humble expression of true, simple sympathy. Only a rural community such as this could give so much. Their extension of our sorrow seemed to magnify the loss of the whole community.

When it was all over, we were left in our grief, disappointment, and continuing sorrow. Time itself was hardly a tonic for the loss we bore. We tried to resolve that many families had lost their precious sons in the last years of the war. Then we tried to compare our loss to what the Russians, English, French, and yes even the Germans and Japanese had to deal with when the common denominator of those became "one" to those families.

Our central Minnesota "country" family needed some special counseling badly, in order to deal with just finding ourselves again. But there was none. My parents looked to the Clergy, but there was very little comfort in the shallow verbiage that was offered.

We had so much grain in the field, cut and stacked. In a few days the Threshing Crew would be at our place. Dad was still devastated by the events just a few days earlier. This strong person, "our beacon", was barely able to work or do anything meaningful.

I knew as a boy of eleven that it was up to Erv and I, to work as we never had before. The threshers came, and the harvest began. The harvest was heavy. In fact it was the heaviest we had ever seen. It surpassed anything ever before on that rock laden farm in central Morrison County! At one point in the afternoon, Dad asked me how I was holding up? Getting tired? "Yes, but okay." I was hauling double grain wagons from the rented farms back to the granary on our home place with the new tractor. I must have hauled twenty loads (in ten trips). My heart skipped a beat when I saw my Uncle John coming up the state road with his Case Tractor and grain wagons. I never had a better uncle in the world because he came to help us when he knew we were in such great need.

We ended up with grain in every available space and had to haul away 800 more bushels of oats to the local Co-op. When the harvesting was finally done, my parents went to St. Cloud to visit mother's brothers and sisters.

In the years before the war, life seemed much happier, even if many of the people had very little and it was hard to make ends meet.

I remember plainly, happier times when we went as a family to church picnics. There was always the "Dixville Picnic" where we saw many of the Keehr's that lived around Little Rock. Then in a week or so there was the Ramey Picnic. There were Talberg's, cousin Starr's, Moran's, and many people who always genuinely enjoyed seeing us. The Morrill Fall Festival was another get together where you could always depend on seeing old friends, Stellmach's, Sauer's, Gall's, the list could go on and on. The people were Lutheran and Catholic, but they mingled and had so much fun as they attended and patronized each other's Picnics.

The food! The food was brought by the wives from their kitchens, serving the best chicken dinners you ever tasted, along with special creamy delicious potato salad, baked beans, gelatins, fruit salad, hot dishes of macaroni, and many other surprises. There was always plenty of keg beer for the men, and soft drinks of Nu-Grape, Orange, Seven-Up, Coca-Cola and Root Beer for the ladies and kids. On these Sunday gatherings, one hated to see the day go by so quickly. These were truly magnificent times, especially in the thirties and forties.

I don't think mother and dad were ever the same again after we lost Donald. As much as they cared for us, I believe they just had a lot of difficulty seeing the path beyond the next day. They seemed preoccupied, and their concentration on daily needs, were not focused.

My dad lost his great spirit and recognized his lack of zeal early after harvesting. He totally lost his interest in farming. He just couldn't get back into his old routine anymore. By the 10th of October, he arranged to have an "Auction Sale". He sold everything of any value on the farm, including his horses, the new tractor, all the milk cows, livestock, and farm machinery.

My parents made several trips to the Veterans Administration in St. Cloud in the weeks that followed. They filed the legal papers necessary for insurance pertaining to the death of Donald. Each time, upon returning back to the farm, there was still greater anxiety, and complete indifference as to what needed to be done to face the future necessities of life.

I was eleven years old now and in the sixth grade. Brother Erv, finished grade school in May of 1945. Al was in third grade.

One early fall day, I had a very difficult experience at uncle Tony's place. It was in the third week of September. My parents were scheduled to sign documents in order to collect insurance on the life of Donald. As they were leaving the farm in the car, my dad told me to go over to Tony's and make sure the cattle and horses had water in the stock tank. Then they left for St. Cloud and the Veterans Administration. After finishing, they planned to stop and visit with my mothers' brother, Joe, in Sauk Rapids.

The weather had been very hot for over a month, so the livestock drank a lot of water. There were about 24 youngstock and three horses at the tank when I got there. Every day, somebody had to go and start the gasoline engine attached to the "pumpjack". That would engage the waterpump to fill the water tank for the animals.

The first thing I did was look in the tank and it was bone dry. I had never done the starting of the motor before, but I was about to find out all about it. The cattle were bellowing and the horses were unruly. The Briggs and Stratton motor had a loose rope 'pull starter' that had to be wound up every time to turn the motor over for starting. The motor was connected direct to the pumpjack. I wasn't able to pull hard enough to get the motor started. I worked at it and pulled my guts out but just didn't have the strength to get the motor started.

I looked the situation over, and saw there were four mounting bolts holding the engine in place, keeping the belt tight. I had to get those bolts loosened to be able to start the motor without the cumbersome pumpjack being attached.

I ran back to the farm and brought back a pliers and an adjustable wrench to the scene, and loosened the four bolts, slid the motor forward, and took the belt off the pulleys. Then I was able to get the motor started. Troubles were just beginning as I tried to put the belt back on the motor and pumpjack pulleys. I found a stick, and tried using it as a guide to help get the belt back on, but the belt caught the stick and it flew off in the weeds. I was getting desperate. The engine was running, the animals were very thirsty and unsettled and each time I almost had the belt on, I would lose it. I would try again only to lose it again. Finally, I put the belt on the big pulley, and with the aid of the wrench, I was able to get the belt on the little motor pulley. Now, I still had to draw the belt tight. I was exhausted, and still had to draw the motor back to tighten the belt to get the water to pump. I looked around and found a medium sized straight tree limb. I wedged it against the well planks and was finally able to tighten the motor in place with the water starting to pump.

I never saw gratitude and gratefulness in any living thing like the looks of those big eyes of the animals, when the water started to flow from the pipe of the well to the dry stock tank. The cattle and horses pushed each other out of the way in order to get at the precious water.

What a hard lesson. Nothing was ever easy. As an eleven year old, I had all the farming I ever wanted! Those were the days of kerosene lamps and lanterns in the house and in the barn. Also before refrigerators, or electricity. There was word that the R.E.A. (Rural Electric Association) had plans to bring electrical service into the area, but it would not begin for several more years.

The weather turned cold on Thanksgiving Day in 1945. As we sat down for our dinner that day we could hardly understand what happened when the war ended, and we sat in disbelief at the course our lives had taken.

A few days later, after school, I walked about a half mile north of the school on the state road to the farm to see "Bobby", the big horse. He was my favorite horse. I expected to see him in the pasture of his new owner. Bobby was sold in October at the Auction Sale to a farmer who lived just north of the school. As I approached the snow covered pasture, I saw three horses. One of them was Bobby.

He saw me and came right over to the fence alongside the road. I talked to him, and petted his face and neck. He looked different to me because he had his winter coat of fur. He would need it. This would be his first winter as an “outside horse”. From as long as I can remember, dad always kept the horses in the barn in the winter, especially at night.

Despite his size, he had a trot and gallop that was as smooth as silk. I remember whenever I rode on his back (never with a saddle), I would hang onto his mane in order not to fall off. He was the most gentle animal I ever knew. I couldn’t stay any longer because I was getting too cold, so I wished him well, and said a feeble goodbye to still another “friend”.

An unusual thing happened just a few days before Christmas, 1945. One day, my dad came home from the Little Rock Store, and brought a box full of used ice skates into the house. My brothers and I dug through the box to try to find something that would fit. I ended up finding nothing that I liked or that fit, except one unlikely pair that kept getting in the way. I wasn't even considering them because they were not "Hard Toe" Hockey Skates. Instead, they were a dirty white pair, with thin chrome blades and little sharp jagged teeth in the front. I was more than displeased with the looks of them as I tried them on, but at least they fit my feet.

On the following Sunday, my cousins took us ice skating on a pond a few miles from our house, and that's when I found out my skates were called "figure skates". It was a blessing in disguise, as I learned to skate. I found myself in the years to follow, doing many maneuvers on those skates. What started out as not very much to my liking, turned out for me to be able to skate with beauty and grace.

A young Dick Button was skating, practicing his routine for the Olympics, on figure skates and I was happy I found them in that unlikely box of old used skates. Dick Button went on to become one of the most influencial skaters in history, and propelling the art into one of the most enjoyable programs ever in spectator events. I felt privileged to be able to foster thoughts of his talents when I skated my best.

Life on the farm seemed far removed from the days when we all contributed and worked so hard to get all the work done each day. There was fulfillment in attending to the milk cows and livestock, even though the work was not glamorous by any means. Just the fact that that we knew we had taken good care of those animals, allowed a sense of giving gratitude to these innocent and dependent animals.

Now, after the animals were all sold and in other farmer's possessions, I often wondered if they received the same kind care and respect as they did from us. My dad was a very kind and patient man, and treated his animals with respect. He also taught us boys to practice the same kindness and caring. In the absence of the farm animals, there was something missing, or "hollow".

Days and nights seemed to be absent of "a simple joy of working with one another".

Yes, the hard work was strangely absent, but not for the better. Deep in our hearts, we knew our lives were better and more meaningful when we were busy. Without the meaningful work which we were so accustomed to, we found our thoughts dwelled heavier on a prevailing sorrow. The family was still trying desperately to heal, and busier would have been better.

Mother and dad took more and more trips to the St. Cloud area. Mother found some consolation in being with her brothers, Joe and Frank, and sisters, Susan and Genevieve, and that was good. It was on one of those trips they found a house to buy in Sauk Rapids, not far from Uncle Joe.

The family spent our last Christmas and New Year on the farm, and there was very little discussion about thoughts of moving off the farm, even though there was very little left with the exception of the memories of happier times. It seemed as though there was a fear of the "unknown" with regard to the contemplative thought of tearing up our old roots and trying to resettle. At some point, we all felt a sense of insecurity when we talked about moving,

As January gave way to February, the moving day was finally decided. The house my parents bought was to be vacant and unoccupied as of February 24th.

During the month of February the family was making preparations to move. The plans were more mental than physical, if one realizes. The physical belongings did not amount to a real lot. We still had mixed emotions about leaving Little Rock, but we knew we could no longer stay on the farm. For the most part, we all knew and agreed that moving to Sauk Rapids would help to give us a new lease on life. It would be an opportunity to turn the page; so to speak; and provide a chance to start life anew.

On the last day of school at District 115, I bid my schoolmates goodbye. It was not easy saying goodbye again. I liked my schoolmates, each and every one. Even though I did not have a strong liking for the teacher, I respected her and felt she did her best. The passing of time put a greater distance since Miss Hegg and Miss Kaiser, whom I felt were so very good for us. Their spirit still lived in the brick, one room schoolhouse, District 115.

Chapter Seven: The End of an Era

On February 25th, 1946, my dad backed our faithful old two-wheeled trailer to the steps of the house. There were things we were not taking: for example, the old wood fired cookstove, the old round table, and the "airtight heater". We managed to pack three beds and mattresses, the kitchen table and chairs, and two chests of drawers on the trailer. Mother and dad carefully packed fruit jars of canned meats, peaches, (and whatever other canned corn, tomatoes, peas and beans that were stored in the cellar pantry), into the trunk of the car, so we would have food at our new house.

It was after 6:00 PM when we finally pulled out of the yard. It was the end of an era. My brothers, Erv and Al sat in the back seat, with our family cattle Dog, "Rex", and a sack of potatoes, next to me. About 25 miles to the south, awaited our new home. My dad drove slowly as we turned the corner to go south from Little Rock. From this point on, the road was blacktop all the rest of the way.

From early on, The Keehr Family name was well known around Little Rock. In fact, as a very little boy, I knew Matt Keehr and Gene Keehr when they managed the Little Rock Co-op and sold 100 pound sacks of flour, egg mash, and ground feed at the store. Just across the road from the town of Little Rock, lived Herbert "Shine" Keehr. He and his good wife had three children, Lloyd, LaVonne, and Gerald (Jerry). On the many occasions of Picnics that were held at the little Dixville Lutheran Church, (a short distance from Little Rock), we would always look for Lloyd and Jerry. They were fun to be with. There were other Keehr families as well. There was Oscar Keehr, and John Keehr. My dad always held the Keehr's in high regard because they were very honest and helpful people.

I thought about Little Rock as we rode in the car, about the storekeepers, Britz and Kowitz. They were a part of my young life, and I had many Cherrio Icc Cream bars, out of the cold box that stood alongside the main counter of the store. This was the store where my parents bought many of our food items for as long as I can remember.

We were unaware of it at the time we moved, but not long after we moved to town, the Herbert (Shine) Keehr family also moved from Little Rock to Sauk Rapids. Their presence seemed to fortify and bring reassurance to our own "settling in". In the years that followed, "Shine", as he was known, became the "head custodian" at the high school, and his good deeds made him the most admired person in the entire administration.

We arrived with our fully loaded trailer just after nightfall. Immediately we started to unload everything we had into the house.

I was surprised to learn that the house sat on top of the highest hill in town, next to the Water Tower. Our neighbors just south over the fence, were the Poor Sisters of St Clare. The "Poor Clare's" live in a reclusive Monastery community, with it's lovely Chapel and Gardens.

The house had electricity, a bathroom, running hot and cold water, a refrigerator, gas stove, a coal fired furnace, heated upstairs, and an attached double garage. As we looked over the City of St. Cloud from high above, we saw all the lights aglow to the southwest, across the Mississippi River.

My mom and dad hugged each other and they put their arms around us as we looked at all the bright lights against the deep dark blue night sky. For a few precious moments, we looked with wonder and shared their joy! Something wonderful had happened.

We knew at that moment, we had found our new home. It was the final gift, a most precious gift we received from Donald. The life insurance on Donald, provided my parents with the means to afford this change in our lives.

Whether or not everybody knew it, Donald would not have wanted it any other way. Tomorrow the sun will shine into our lives once again.

The very next day, our good dog, "Rex" disappeared. We could find no trace of him.

Three days later, we received word from the new people on the farm. "The dog came back to the farm"!

An incredible feat. Dad said, "I hope you will keep him and take good care of him. He's a good faithful dog, and he needs to be on the farm. That's where his heart is!" And, so they did!

I didn't realize he was looking and watching out of the car window the night we moved.

How else would Rex know which direction would lead him twenty five miles back to the farm?

A miracle, perhaps?

The End

Epilogue

As it is, so many times, books remain in the dark, and shrouded in secret until a reader comes along and sheds light onto the written pages. Only then, does the book become immortal. Bound between the covers of books, are the thoughts and dreams of new and age-old talented writers. We cannot help but learn from the wisdom of these literary efforts.

It would be my ambition and desire, that this book would hold the reader with interest and intensity, as I lived during the days of my formative years .

Ralph Waldo Emerson said: "T' is the Reader that makes a Good Book !"

Good reading !

Acknowledgement

I would like to thank

Maurice Faust and Liane Bonin

for their generous and unselfish help

in getting this book published.